PROJECT:

TO DO:

☐

☐

☐

☐

☐

☐

☐

☐

☐

☐

COMPLETE!

PROJECT:

NOTES:

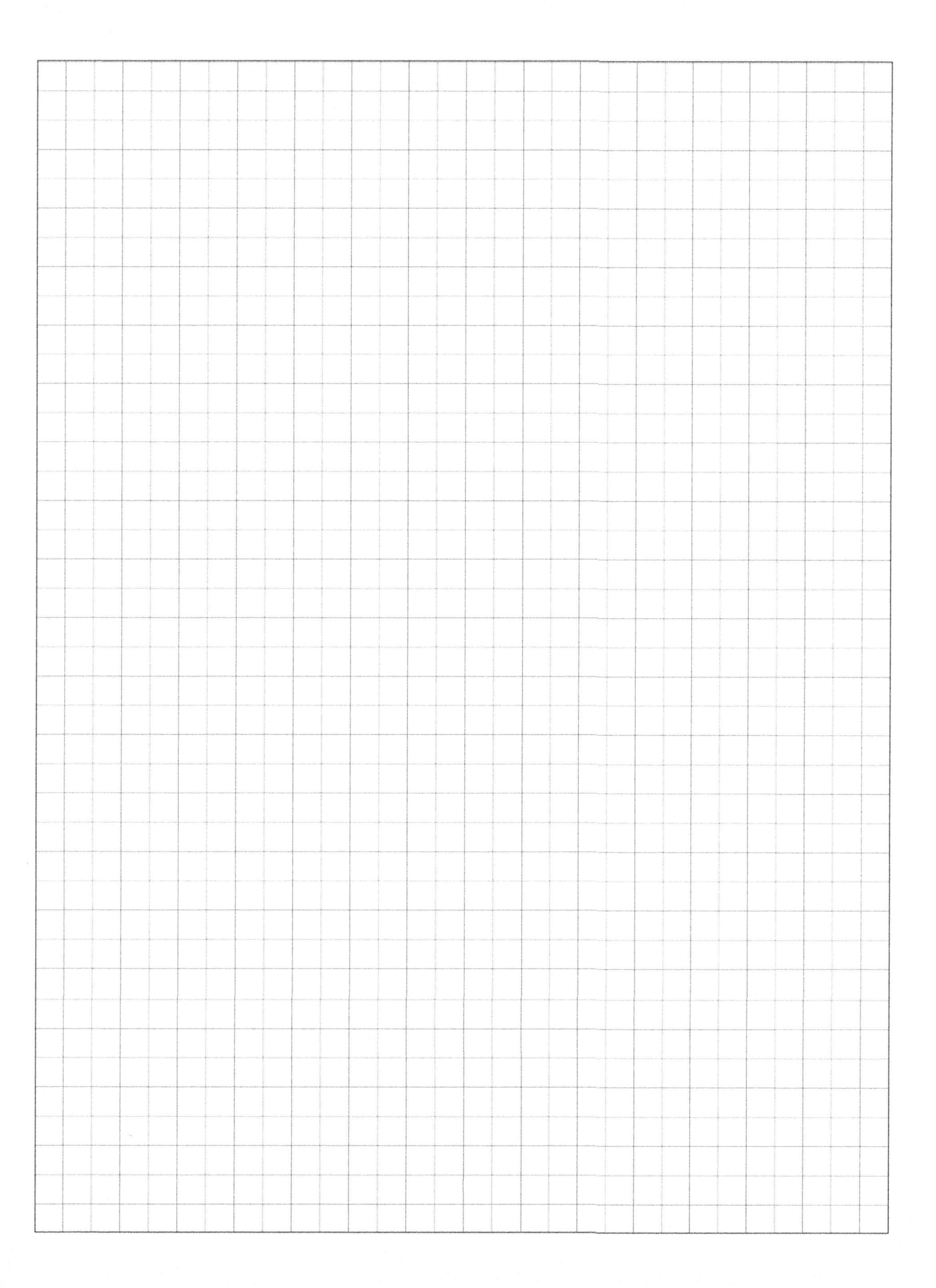

PROJECT BUDGET			
ITEM	SOURCE	COST	✓
	TOTAL:		

FINISHES + DETAILS		
PAINT BRAND	COLOR + LOCATION	FINISH + INT/EXT
TILE BRAND	TILE SOURCE	COLOR + LOCATION
FLOORING SOURCE/BRAND	MATERIAL	COLOR/CODE
COUNTER SOURCE/BRAND	MATERIAL	COLOR/CODE
CABINET SOURCE/BRAND	MATERIAL	COLOR/FINISH
APPLIANCE	BRAND	COLOR/FINISH
LIGHTING SOURCE/BRAND	INSTALL LOCATION	COLOR/FINISH

CONTRACTOR QUOTES + CONTACT
COMPANY:
PHONE: EMAIL:
JOB: NOTES:
PRICE:
COMPANY:
PHONE: EMAIL:
JOB: NOTES:
PRICE:
COMPANY:
PHONE: EMAIL:
JOB: NOTES:
PRICE:
COMPANY:
PHONE: EMAIL:
JOB: NOTES:
PRICE:

FINAL PUNCH LIST:	NOTES:
☐	
☐	
☐	
☐	
☐	
☐	
☐	
☐	
☐	
☐	
☐	

BRAINSTORM:

BRAINSTORM:

PROJECT:

TO DO:

☐

☐

☐

☐

☐

☐

☐

☐

☐

☐

COMPLETE!

PROJECT:

NOTES:

PROJECT BUDGET			
ITEM	SOURCE	COST	✓
	TOTAL:		

FINISHES + DETAILS		
PAINT BRAND	COLOR + LOCATION	FINISH + INT/EXT
TILE BRAND	TILE SOURCE	COLOR + LOCATION
FLOORING SOURCE/BRAND	MATERIAL	COLOR/CODE
COUNTER SOURCE/BRAND	MATERIAL	COLOR/CODE
CABINET SOURCE/BRAND	MATERIAL	COLOR/FINISH
APPLIANCE	BRAND	COLOR/FINISH
LIGHTING SOURCE/BRAND	INSTALL LOCATION	COLOR/FINISH

CONTRACTOR QUOTES + CONTACT

COMPANY:	
PHONE:	EMAIL:
JOB:	NOTES:
PRICE:	

COMPANY:	
PHONE:	EMAIL:
JOB:	NOTES:
PRICE:	

COMPANY:	
PHONE:	EMAIL:
JOB:	NOTES:
PRICE:	

COMPANY:	
PHONE:	EMAIL:
JOB:	NOTES:
PRICE:	

FINAL PUNCH LIST:	NOTES:
☐	
☐	
☐	
☐	
☐	
☐	
☐	
☐	
☐	
☐	
☐	
FINAL PUNCH LIST:	NOTES:

BRAINSTORM:

PROJECT:

TO DO:

☐

☐

☐

☐

☐

☐

☐

☐

☐

☐

COMPLETE!

PROJECT:

NOTES:

PROJECT BUDGET			
ITEM	SOURCE	COST	✓
	TOTAL:		
ITEM	SOURCE	COST	

FINISHES + DETAILS		
PAINT BRAND	COLOR + LOCATION	FINISH + INT/EXT
TILE BRAND	TILE SOURCE	COLOR + LOCATION
FLOORING SOURCE/BRAND	MATERIAL	COLOR/CODE
COUNTER SOURCE/BRAND	MATERIAL	COLOR/CODE
CABINET SOURCE/BRAND	MATERIAL	COLOR/FINISH
APPLIANCE	BRAND	COLOR/FINISH
LIGHTING SOURCE/BRAND	INSTALL LOCATION	COLOR/FINISH

CONTRACTOR QUOTES + CONTACT	
COMPANY:	
PHONE:	EMAIL:
JOB:	NOTES:
PRICE:	
COMPANY:	
PHONE:	EMAIL:
JOB:	NOTES:
PRICE:	
COMPANY:	
PHONE:	EMAIL:
JOB:	NOTES:
PRICE:	
COMPANY:	
PHONE:	EMAIL:
JOB:	NOTES:
PRICE:	

FINAL PUNCH LIST:	NOTES:
☐	
☐	
☐	
☐	
☐	
☐	
☐	
☐	
☐	
☐	
☐	
FINAL PUNCH LIST:	NOTES:

BRAINSTORM:

BRAINSTORM:

PROJECT:

TO DO:

- [ ]
- [ ]
- [ ]
- [ ]
- [ ]
- [ ]
- [ ]
- [ ]
- [ ]
- [ ]

COMPLETE!

PROJECT:

NOTES:

PROJECT BUDGET			
ITEM	SOURCE	COST	✓
	TOTAL:		

FINISHES + DETAILS		
PAINT BRAND	COLOR + LOCATION	FINISH + INT/EXT
TILE BRAND	TILE SOURCE	COLOR + LOCATION
FLOORING SOURCE/BRAND	MATERIAL	COLOR/CODE
COUNTER SOURCE/BRAND	MATERIAL	COLOR/CODE
CABINET SOURCE/BRAND	MATERIAL	COLOR/FINISH
APPLIANCE	BRAND	COLOR/FINISH
LIGHTING SOURCE/BRAND	INSTALL LOCATION	COLOR/FINISH

CONTRACTOR QUOTES + CONTACT	
COMPANY:	
PHONE:	EMAIL:
JOB:	NOTES:
PRICE:	
COMPANY:	
PHONE:	EMAIL:
JOB:	NOTES:
PRICE:	
COMPANY:	
PHONE:	EMAIL:
JOB:	NOTES:
PRICE:	
COMPANY:	
PHONE:	EMAIL:
JOB:	NOTES:
PRICE:	

FINAL PUNCH LIST: NOTES:

BRAINSTORM:

PROJECT:

TO DO:

☐

☐

☐

☐

☐

☐

☐

☐

☐

☐

COMPLETE!

PROJECT:

NOTES:

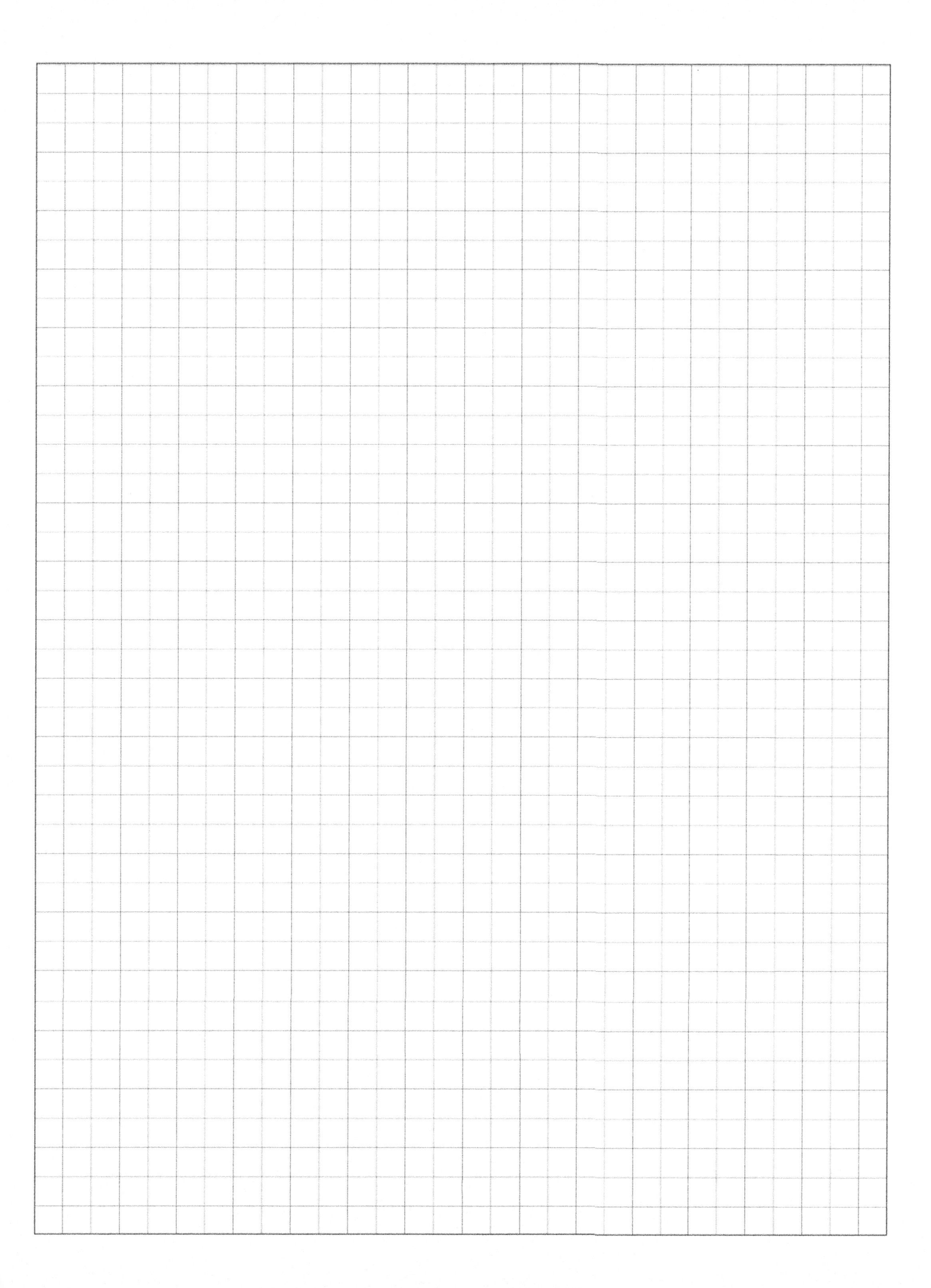

PROJECT BUDGET			
ITEM	SOURCE	COST	✓
	TOTAL:		

FINISHES + DETAILS		
PAINT BRAND	COLOR + LOCATION	FINISH + INT/EXT
TILE BRAND	TILE SOURCE	COLOR + LOCATION
FLOORING SOURCE/BRAND	MATERIAL	COLOR/CODE
COUNTER SOURCE/BRAND	MATERIAL	COLOR/CODE
CABINET SOURCE/BRAND	MATERIAL	COLOR/FINISH
APPLIANCE	BRAND	COLOR/FINISH
LIGHTING SOURCE/BRAND	INSTALL LOCATION	COLOR/FINISH

CONTRACTOR QUOTES + CONTACT

COMPANY:

PHONE:	EMAIL:
JOB:	NOTES:
PRICE:	

COMPANY:

PHONE:	EMAIL:
JOB:	NOTES:
PRICE:	

COMPANY:

PHONE:	EMAIL:
JOB:	NOTES:
PRICE:	

COMPANY:

PHONE:	EMAIL:
JOB:	NOTES:
PRICE:	

FINAL PUNCH LIST:	NOTES:
☐	
☐	
☐	
☐	
☐	
☐	
☐	
☐	
☐	
☐	
☐	

BRAINSTORM:

BRAINSTORM:

PROJECT:

TO DO:

COMPLETE!

PROJECT:

NOTES:

PROJECT BUDGET			
ITEM	SOURCE	COST	✓
	TOTAL:		

FINISHES + DETAILS		
PAINT BRAND	COLOR + LOCATION	FINISH + INT/EXT
TILE BRAND	TILE SOURCE	COLOR + LOCATION
FLOORING SOURCE/BRAND	MATERIAL	COLOR/CODE
COUNTER SOURCE/BRAND	MATERIAL	COLOR/CODE
CABINET SOURCE/BRAND	MATERIAL	COLOR/FINISH
APPLIANCE	BRAND	COLOR/FINISH
LIGHTING SOURCE/BRAND	INSTALL LOCATION	COLOR/FINISH

CONTRACTOR QUOTES + CONTACT

COMPANY:

PHONE: **EMAIL:**

JOB: **NOTES:**

PRICE:

COMPANY:

PHONE: **EMAIL:**

JOB: **NOTES:**

PRICE:

COMPANY:

PHONE: **EMAIL:**

JOB: **NOTES:**

PRICE:

COMPANY:

PHONE: **EMAIL:**

JOB: **NOTES:**

PRICE:

FINAL PUNCH LIST:	NOTES:
☐	
☐	
☐	
☐	
☐	
☐	
☐	
☐	
☐	
☐	
☐	

BRAINSTORM:

PROJECT:

TO DO:

☐	☐
☐	☐
☐	☐
☐	☐
☐	☐

COMPLETE!

PROJECT:

NOTES:

PROJECT BUDGET			
ITEM	SOURCE	COST	✓
	TOTAL:		

FINISHES + DETAILS		
PAINT BRAND	COLOR + LOCATION	FINISH + INT/EXT
TILE BRAND	TILE SOURCE	COLOR + LOCATION
FLOORING SOURCE/BRAND	MATERIAL	COLOR/CODE
COUNTER SOURCE/BRAND	MATERIAL	COLOR/CODE
CABINET SOURCE/BRAND	MATERIAL	COLOR/FINISH
APPLIANCE	BRAND	COLOR/FINISH
LIGHTING SOURCE/BRAND	INSTALL LOCATION	COLOR/FINISH

CONTRACTOR QUOTES + CONTACT	
COMPANY:	
PHONE:	EMAIL:
JOB:	NOTES:
PRICE:	
COMPANY:	
PHONE:	EMAIL:
JOB:	NOTES:
PRICE:	
COMPANY:	
PHONE:	EMAIL:
JOB:	NOTES:
PRICE:	
COMPANY:	
PHONE:	EMAIL:
JOB:	NOTES:
PRICE:	

FINAL PUNCH LIST:

- [ ]
- [ ]
- [ ]
- [ ]
- [ ]
- [ ]
- [ ]
- [ ]
- [ ]
- [ ]
- [ ]

NOTES:

BRAINSTORM:

BRAINSTORM:

PROJECT:

TO DO:

COMPLETE!

PROJECT:

NOTES:

PROJECT BUDGET				
ITEM	SOURCE	COST	✓
	TOTAL:		

FINISHES + DETAILS		
PAINT BRAND	COLOR + LOCATION	FINISH + INT/EXT
TILE BRAND	TILE SOURCE	COLOR + LOCATION
FLOORING SOURCE/BRAND	MATERIAL	COLOR/CODE
COUNTER SOURCE/BRAND	MATERIAL	COLOR/CODE
CABINET SOURCE/BRAND	MATERIAL	COLOR/FINISH
APPLIANCE	BRAND	COLOR/FINISH
LIGHTING SOURCE/BRAND	INSTALL LOCATION	COLOR/FINISH

CONTRACTOR QUOTES + CONTACT

COMPANY:

PHONE:	EMAIL:
JOB:	NOTES:
PRICE:	

COMPANY:

PHONE:	EMAIL:
JOB:	NOTES:
PRICE:	

COMPANY:

PHONE:	EMAIL:
JOB:	NOTES:
PRICE:	

COMPANY:

PHONE:	EMAIL:
JOB:	NOTES:
PRICE:	

FINAL PUNCH LIST:

- [ ]
- [ ]
- [ ]
- [ ]
- [ ]
- [ ]
- [ ]
- [ ]
- [ ]
- [ ]
- [ ]

NOTES:

BRAINSTORM:

BRAINSTORM:

PROJECT:

TO DO:

COMPLETE!

PROJECT:

NOTES:

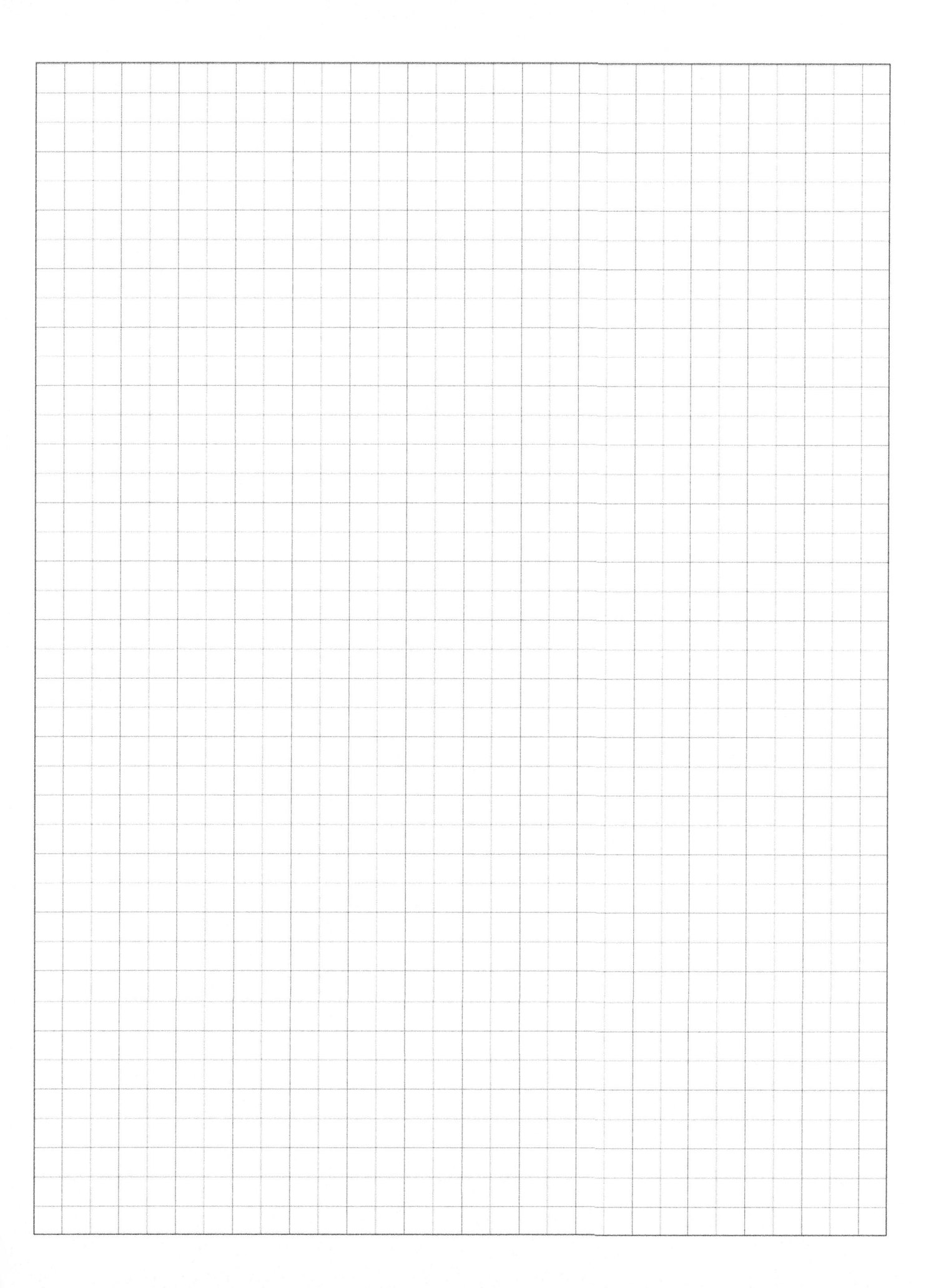

PROJECT BUDGET				
ITEM	SOURCE	COST	✓
	TOTAL:		
ITEM	SOURCE	COST	

FINISHES + DETAILS		
PAINT BRAND	COLOR + LOCATION	FINISH + INT/EXT
TILE BRAND	TILE SOURCE	COLOR + LOCATION
FLOORING SOURCE/BRAND	MATERIAL	COLOR/CODE
COUNTER SOURCE/BRAND	MATERIAL	COLOR/CODE
CABINET SOURCE/BRAND	MATERIAL	COLOR/FINISH
APPLIANCE	BRAND	COLOR/FINISH
LIGHTING SOURCE/BRAND	INSTALL LOCATION	COLOR/FINISH

CONTRACTOR QUOTES + CONTACT

COMPANY:

PHONE: EMAIL:

JOB: NOTES:

PRICE:

COMPANY:

PHONE: EMAIL:

JOB: NOTES:

PRICE:

COMPANY:

PHONE: EMAIL:

JOB: NOTES:

PRICE:

COMPANY:

PHONE: EMAIL:

JOB: NOTES:

PRICE:

FINAL PUNCH LIST:	NOTES:
☐	
☐	
☐	
☐	
☐	
☐	
☐	
☐	
☐	
☐	
☐	

BRAINSTORM:

BRAINSTORM:

PROJECT:

TO DO:

☐	☐
☐	☐
☐	☐
☐	☐
☐	☐

COMPLETE!

PROJECT:

NOTES:

PROJECT BUDGET			
ITEM	SOURCE	COST	✓
	TOTAL:		
ITEM	SOURCE	COST	

FINISHES + DETAILS		
PAINT BRAND	COLOR + LOCATION	FINISH + INT/EXT
TILE BRAND	TILE SOURCE	COLOR + LOCATION
FLOORING SOURCE/BRAND	MATERIAL	COLOR/CODE
COUNTER SOURCE/BRAND	MATERIAL	COLOR/CODE
CABINET SOURCE/BRAND	MATERIAL	COLOR/FINISH
APPLIANCE	BRAND	COLOR/FINISH
LIGHTING SOURCE/BRAND	INSTALL LOCATION	COLOR/FINISH

| CONTRACTOR QUOTES + CONTACT |

COMPANY:

PHONE: | EMAIL:

JOB: | NOTES:
PRICE: |

COMPANY:

PHONE: | EMAIL:

JOB: | NOTES:
PRICE: |

COMPANY:

PHONE: | EMAIL:

JOB: | NOTES:
PRICE: |

COMPANY:

PHONE: | EMAIL:

JOB: | NOTES:
PRICE: |

FINAL PUNCH LIST:

- [ ]
- [ ]
- [ ]
- [ ]
- [ ]
- [ ]
- [ ]
- [ ]
- [ ]
- [ ]
- [ ]

NOTES:

BRAINSTORM:

BRAINSTORM:

Made in the USA
Monee, IL
06 November 2022